EI

Understand And Master
Own Powers

MATTHEW BRIGHTHOUSE

Copyright © 2018

Table of Contents

INTRODUCTION..3

1 ENFJ 101..6

2 USE YOUR SKILLS TO HELP THE UNDERDOG 13

3 USE YOUR CARING ATTITUDE TO MAKE A DIFFERENCE 18

4 LEARN TO TAP INTO YOUR INTUITION 21

5 DEVELOP YOUR LEADERSHIP SKILLS.....................................28

6 USE YOUR CHARISMA AND OUTGOING NATURE TO SOCIALIZE AND NETWORK 33

CONCLUSION...37

Introduction

The ability to learn about yourself and address your strengths and weaknesses is a very worthwhile journey for all of us to go on. This is the number one way to not only achieve your potential, but smash it too! We all have ups and downs in life, but what's important is being able to recognize that we all have the power to take control of what we take from the experience.

By picking up this book you have shown a willingness to find out about your own personality type. From what makes you tick, your core personality traits, your strengths, your weaknesses, and what types of jobs are suited to you. All of this information is unlocked simply by taking the Myers-Briggs personality test, and getting your final result.

The fact you have chosen this particular book tells us that you are an ENFJ. You're an enigma that's for sure, because you make up only 2% of the overall population! There is nobody quite like you, and that's a major plus point in your direction!

Throughout this book we are going to explore the wonderful world of the ENFJ, and we're going to give you hints, tips, and suggestions on how you can take those positive traits you have (and there are many), and then help you push them further forward. This will give you the greatest chance possible of being the best version of yourself that you can be. Why would you want to be anything else?

Of course, learning about personalities overall is a truly interesting subject. Whether you're a manager, a counsellor, or just someone who enjoys learning about psychology and what makes people tick, understanding more about the different personality types within the spectrum, will help you understand people on a much deeper level overall. This will enhance your management endeavors, if that is your role, and it will also help you form deeper bonds with those around you. Getting to the core of why someone acts the way they do, will help you become closer, and not edge away because you simply don't 'get it'.

By the end of this book you will truly 'get' your ENFJ nature, that's for sure!

We do need to point out that there is not one person on this planet who is 100% their particular personality type. We are all slightly different in our make-up, and we have all experienced things in our lives which have changed us slightly and altered our outlook. Whilst our core personality remains the same, it does have a slight altering effect on how we see the world, as well as how we react to situations. For that reason, you might not recognize yourself in every single one of the areas we talk about as we move through the book. Don't worry! There is nothing wrong with you! It's simply that you haven't unearthed every part of your personality yet, and that's where the fun really does start! Discovering your strengths is just as much a part of this journey as enhancing the ones you already have!

Be sure to read through the other personality types which you feel you may have a connection with too. It could very well be that you are on the cusp in a few different ways, and by knowing more about the other types, you could further enhance your self-discovery journey. For example, some people find that they are on the borderline between extrovert and introvert. This is completely normal, as human beings cannot truly be categorized into a bunch of letters. We are all way more unique than that.

Every single part of this book is aimed towards positivity and change for the better. Do not take any part of this book personality in a negative way, because that's certainly not the way it is intended. We're not focusing on weaknesses here, although it's important to realize that we are all flawed human beings from the day we're born, and that means that of course we have negatives sides to our personalities – we're only human! By understanding that point, you will come to a more satisfied and balanced place; you can simply work on those at a later date. For now, we're focusing 100% on our strengths! Let's celebrate the positive side of our personality, and let's work on pushing it even further forward, so we can unlock the potential of those strengths, and achieve greater happiness and success in the future.

Enough talking, let's get on with it. Grab a pen and paper, sit somewhere quiet, and be prepared to be wowed by the wonder and outgoing nature of the ENFJ personality type.

If you'd like to learn more about developing your weaknesses, you can get my other book - [ENFJ: Understand And Break Free From Your Own Limitations.](#) But for now, let's get back to business and focus on your powers.

1
ENFJ 101

So, you're an ENFJ! That means you're certainly one of the world's good guys. That means you're always looking to stand up for the little man, the one who is struggling, the underdog. You're a great speaker, you're confident, you're charismatic, but you're also a kind individual, someone who is often well-liked, and super-reliable to boot.

You sound a pretty stand-up kind of guy or girl, right?

That's because you are!

This book is all about celebrating strengths and understanding how you can maximize their effects, to give you greater gains in the future. Of course, these gains might not only affect you, but those around you too. For instance, we're going to talk in a later chapter about how you're someone who can really make a difference to others, because you have a very in-depth need to stand up for those who are struggling. Not only will pushing that skill to a greater degree make you feel good about yourself and increase your confidence, but it is going to have greater outcomes for the people you're trying to help. Double whammy of positivity!

So, let's get down to it.

Every single personality type in the Myers-Briggs spectrum has four letters to symbolize the personality type's main headers. In your case, those letters are E,

N, F, and J. They may not mean anything to you at this point, so let's break it down and explore what they mean, and what they stand for.

E – Extraversion
N – Intuition
F – Feeling
J – Judgement

The E for extraversion means that you are an outgoing, social kind of person. You're not a wallflower, you're not a doormat, you're nobody's puppet. Whilst you're a strong person however, you are quite sensitive, and you do tend to take things to heart. That is what keeps you grounded and stops you from becoming overbearing. The perfect blend in so many ways.

Your extroversion also makes you the ideal person to help others. You like to talk to people, you like to know about them, and if you find that there is a cause you can help with, you'll be on-board 100%. This also works well with the N part of your personality make up. The N actually stands for intuition, and later in this book we're going to give you a lot of advice on how to learn to use your intuition as a guide, and to allow it to help you make important decisions. This is a truly positive skill, and it also helps you to be very genuine and real with those around you. The ENFJ is a very genuine person, literally what you see is what you get, but they are also very good at understanding the motives of other people, by reading between the lines. This is something you can use your intuition to further push this skill to greater levels.

The F stands for feeling. Again, this works well with your intuition, because it gives you compassion, and it gives you confidence to stand up for what is right. You make your decisions with a mixture of gut feeling (intuition), and logic. You like to weigh up the facts, the pros and cons, and use that in line with what you really think about a subject, before you come to a final decision. This also overlaps with the J part of your personality type.

The J stands for judgement. You are someone who doesn't like unfair decisions, you don't like to see injustice. Don't worry, this doesn't make you a judgmental person by any means, it simply eludes to the fact that you use your logic, you understand people, you like to delve into things, before you really come to conclusions or decisions on others, and yourself.

Those are the four letters which make up your particular personality type, and the traits which they pertain to. Of course, that is only a fraction of the story, because within each of those letters is another subsection to belong to it. As we mentioned earlier, you might not totally recognize yourself within those letters at this point. You're unlikely to be nodding along, thinking 'yes, that's totally me' at this point. That is the whole reason we are going on this journey – because currently you might not know what makes your personality tick. It's a complicated mix to unravel!

At this point, you simply need to be open minded, because the more you delve, the more you explore and the more you really think about what makes you tick, the more you will see that these traits really are inside you, and they simply need to be awoken. From there, you can develop them, and the sky really is the limit!

Now we know what the letters stand for, let's learn more about strengths, and to balance it up, a little about weaknesses too.

ENFJ Strengths

This book is totally about strengths, and that is the main focus of what we are talking about. Having said that, balance is important, and to really understand yourself and your type, you need to know about the pros and the cons. In this section, we're going to talk about the common ENFJ strengths, but for completeness sake, we also need to mention the common weaknesses too. Just a mention however!

Of course, not all weaknesses really are weaknesses, it totally depends on the context in which they are being experienced! Because a weakness with an awareness is simply an opportunity to grow from.

Common ENFJ Weaknesses

- A tendency to be a little too idealistic at times
- Can be too selfless, and put themselves last
- Can be too sensitive at times
- Fluctuating self-esteem, due to sensitivity issues
- Can sometimes be indecisive when it comes to the big decisions that need to be made
- Too much empathy at times

As you can see, there is nothing particular terrible in there. If you look at it closely, those really are the traits of someone who cares!

Learning to work on your weaknesses as much as your strengths is certainly something you should do, to really develop your personality as a whole. That's for another book however!

Common ENFJ Strengths

- Very tolerant and open minded in all situations
- A great team player, someone you would want on your side
- Packed with charisma, has a magnetic personality
- Always looking to do good deeds
- A natural born leader
- Inspiring to others
- Authentic, what you see is what you get

You should be patting yourself on the back at this point, as these are great strengths to have! Of course, you might not notice them within yourself right now, and as we mentioned before, it could very well be that they are there (it's very likely), but that you need to do some developmental work to unearth them, and then maximize their potential. That's what this entire journey is about!

In fact, before you continue. Why don't you grab a pen and paper and jot down your own biggest strengths and weaknesses? You can see which ones you are strongly connected to. And you may even notice a handful of others.

As we move on with the book, we're going to be picking out a particular strength and showing you how you can maximize its effects. This is going to allow you to improve yourself overall, but also probably make a great difference in the lives of those around you too.

To give you an idea of the type of effect that an ENFJ has, we need to mention a few famous celebrities who fall within this category. You are keeping great company, because to name just two famous ENFJ's, we have Barack Obama, and Oprah Winfrey. Think of the great work those two have done, and the impact they have had on the lives of many.

Yes, my friend, that could be you too!

Potential Job Matches For an ENFJ

You don't have to go around being a former US President or a famous chat show host turned world-changer to make a difference. There are many jobs which are ideally suited to the skills and personality of an ENFJ, many of which will allow you to make the difference you crave to make, whilst also satisfying your own needs too.

You are known as the 'Protagonist' within your personality type, so it makes sense that the following types of jobs are ideal for the ENFJ:

- Social worker
- Counsellor
- Politician

- Public relations officer/worker
- Teacher
- Fundraiser
- HR manager or specialist
- Psychologist

You can see a common theme emerging within that list – these are all jobs which are not only interesting and have great scope for future growth, but they also focus on helping and guiding others. Is there a new career path within that list that you'd like to take? If you're unhappy in your current role, it's never too late to change direction and start again! It could very well be that you're unsatisfied in your role because it doesn't fulfil the part of you that craves to help others and make a difference.

Now we've really explored the basics of the ENFJ personality type, it's time to get practical. The following chapters are going to pick out a strength and focus entirely on it for that section. We're going to show you how you can learn to maximize the effects of the strength and use it in the future. Remember, if you don't think you have that particular strength in great abundance, that's a sign to really focus on it, and unearth it within you. It's there somewhere. Some strengths may need more work than others, and that's totally fine!

2
Use Your Skills to Help The Underdog

One of the biggest strengths of the ENFJ personality type is a desire and willingness to help others whenever possible. This is something you can use to great effect, and the ironic thing is that by doing this, your self-confidence will soar.

When we do good things for people, we get a hit of satisfaction. This is normal and should never be considered selfish. Of course, your motives for helping someone shouldn't be because you want to feel good about yourself, but it is a pleasant side effect that can have a fantastic knock on effect on the lives of other people.

What a skill to have!

Obviously, that skill can either lay dormant, or it can be developed to great effect. We're all about being proactive and practical, so let's develop it!

You are known as the protagonist, which means that you are an advocate for change, you're someone who wants to help others and achieve positive steps for the future. Your fluctuating self-confidence levels can sometimes be a barrier to this, but it's vital to simply overstep any doubts you have and go for it anyway.

There are many ways you can help others, but you are someone who loves to help the underdog. We're talking about those who don't feel they have a voice, those who are struggling, small businesses who can't compete against the big corporations, that kind of thing. Putting a small example on it, this could be someone who is introverted, perhaps even shy, and struggles to get their very valid point across. As a result, they are forgotten, or their opinion is deemed not to matter. You would take this instance very seriously, and help them get their ideas over, because they matter just as much as anyone else's.

Perhaps someone you know is being bullied at work or in school. You are the ideal person to give them strength, be their voice, and help them overcome these difficult times.

You can be that person, you simply need to know how to do it.

Identify Your Cause
There are millions of causes you could choose, but which is important to you? Not every single cause will call out to the core of you, i.e. you can't help everyone. For that reason, you need to find the causes that really do connect with your values and what you believe to be right. We all have different opinions on right and wrong, so don't be upset that you have to choose just one or two causes – you can't change the world single-handedly!

For instance, if you are someone who loves children and you want to make a difference there, you could look at these two ways. You can either go big, and work with a children's charity on a national or international scale, or you could look at the amount of time that you do have spare, and perhaps go more local. You could volunteer at a children's home, or you could do some fundraising to raise awareness of local issues. On a more personal level, you could help a youngster who is struggling with the troubles of growing up.

The point here is that it doesn't have to be some huge world-changing cause to focus on, it just has to be something that you believe in strongly. By doing that, you will be able to put all of your efforts into it, because you are not someone who gives up easily. You are hard-working and very dedicated, and if you really do believe in something, you will give it your all.

Do remember not to take on too much at once however. You might be tempted to try and help several people or several causes, but you are one person, and you are someone who also needs family time, work time, personal time, you need to sleep! Identify your causes carefully, and that way you will be able to focus on them much more clearly, and much better.

Brainstorm, What Can You Do?

When you first pick a cause to help, there is likely to be two scenarios that could occur. Firstly, you will have a rush of ideas that overwhelm you, and you need to sit and focus on them in order to make sense of what you're thinking about. Or, you might come up with a total blank. There is one solution to both of those scenarios – brainstorm.

Clearing out your mind is a good way to focus and will give you a clearer route forward. So, think about the cause you want to help, grab a piece of paper, and write down everything that comes into your head about it. It doesn't have to be a solution per se, it just needs to be an idea, a thought, something you connect with. Once you've done that, look over the paper and try and form ideas from that. You might need to leave it alone and come back to it a few hours or a few days later, as other ideas might come up in the meantime.

Try asking yourself the following questions…

1. What am I good at?
2. What do I love to do?
3. What do I believe strongly about?
4. Would the closest people in my life give the same answers about me?

The idea is that once you've cleared your mind, you will be able to come up with much more solid and sensible ideas, ones which will work. From there, you identify the idea and you put a plan of action into place.

Don't Give Up

There will always be roadblocks, but you mustn't give up! You are someone who is very dedicated to any cause, but you do have the tendency to either take on too much, or you allow a dip in self-confidence to send you off track. Avoid doing this, and instead, focus on moving forward. You have a great idea, you have a plan, and any movement in the right direction is progress. With every step that leads you towards a good result, you will notice that feeling of satisfaction becoming greater.

Indeed, it might be that your initial plan just isn't work, and in that case, don't abandon it, just change direction! Go back to your brainstorming, as we just talked about, and come up with a new route – you can do it!

Thomas Edison made 1,000 unsuccessful attempts at inventing the first light bulb. Many people would have given up way before then. But he believed in his idea, and the failures became part of the steps to his success.

Keep Pushing For Change

The dedicated and reliable nature of an ENFJ means that you are not likely to stop when you feel like you've reached the end of a particular journey. There's always another to help out, and there is always a way to push for change in a situation. Of course, you should always balance this out with your own time, your own job, your own home situation, but helping others is at the very core of the ENFJ personality type, and if you avoid this, or you don't try and develop this part of your personality, you're not really achieving your potential. You will have a great gift left unexplored, and that gift is not only beneficial to yourself, but to other people too.

Allow your voice to be the one of the underdog, the one who can't get themselves to be heard any other way.

3
Use Your Caring Attitude to Make a Difference

We've talked about causes and how you can help in that regard, but what about being there for those around you?

Being an advocate for change and supporting causes isn't all about the big things in life, it can be about making small changes for those around you too. We mentioned in our last chapter an example about helping someone who is being bullied, being a support system and someone they feel they can go to for help. That is an ideal situation for an ENFJ, because you not only want to help advocate change, but you want to simply be a good friend too.

Put simply, an ENFJ is one of the best friends you can have, because they will never give up on you, and they will always be super-supportive. Use those skills to be a shoulder to cry on. You're also someone who can easily see through to the real motives of someone, because you can tap into your intuition and use it to make informed choices and viewpoints of what is really going on beneath the surface.

Making a difference isn't all about changing the world, it can be about making someone feel better by simply being there or making them smile.

Become a Go-To Support System

In an earlier chapter we talked about some of the best suited jobs for an ENFJ, and amongst those you saw roles like teacher, counsellor, psychologist, sitting comfortably alongside roles such as politician and fundraiser. This shows you the two sides of the situation very clearly – the last two roles we have just mentioned are about helping others on a large scale, whereas the other three are about helping individual in a more personal setting. You can choose, you can do both, it's up to you – whatever you feel comfortable with, and whatever cause really calls out to you.

You can help others every day by simply being a good friend. This doesn't take up a huge amount of time, it isn't a real effort, it's simply about being there for someone when they need you, as you would hope they would be there for you too.

Of course, you shouldn't allow someone to take up too much of your time, e.g. encroach on the time you want to spend with your family, but generally being a good friend is all that is required.

You are someone who is very genuine, someone who is very caring, and these are two of the main strengths pertaining to your personality type. Simply ensuring that people you care about know you're there for them anytime they need you, that is helping others, and that is making a bigger change in their life than you will first realize.

Be an Inspiration

Aside from helping others, ENFJ's love to be an inspiration to others too. You lead by example, and that inspires others to achieve their aims and dreams too. Sometimes you might feel that you're not doing enough, but always be safe in the knowledge that what you do *is* enough, because you put your heart and soul into it.

You have great leadership skills, which we're going to talk about in a later chapter, but one of the easiest ways to lead is to simply be the best version of yourself that you can be, do all you can, and ensure that you're there for others when they need you. This in itself will be an inspiration to others.

This is also about looking at the job you're doing currently. We talked about a few career suggestions earlier in our book, but are you really happy with the job you're in currently? We mentioned that it's never too late to change, so if you're not happy, and there is something you want to do, be brave and go for it! Just make sure that the change is a good one for you, and a positive one for your future. By doing this, you could be an inspiration for someone else close to you who is also unhappy in their job, but they just don't have the fearlessness to go for it. Again, you're inspiring others by leading by example!

You are never afraid to stand up and speak out when you feel something is wrong, or that there is an injustice, so never be afraid to make changes when you feel they need to be made.

4
Learn to Tap Into Your Intuition

You have the 'N' as the second letter in your personality make up, and that stands for 'intuition'. Because it features in the letter section, that means that you have it as a major strength, and if you don't feel that you're a particularly intuition person at this point, it is something you need to work on, because it's certainly in there somewhere!

Many people become confused or even fearful about intuition, because they don't fully understand it. They think it is some psychic skill that is going to somehow connect them to the other side, but that really isn't the case. Yes, intuition is used a lot by mediums, but it is also a quality that many people have generally, and it is nothing to do with tarot cards and crystal balls!

Learning to tap into your intuition, your inner thoughts and feelings, and learning to allow it to guide you, is a real strength you can develop. As we mentioned, it might be that you don't use your intuition too much right now, perhaps out of fear of it, or simply because you don't understand what it is. This particular chapter is going to teach you about intuition and show you how you can allow it to guide you in life's big decisions.

In some ways, you already use your intuition without even realizing it. We talked about the fact that ENFJ's are great at being able to read between the lines and understand someone's real motives. You're not coming to this conclusion through fact alone, some of it comes down to a feeling, something you just know without any real back up. This is your intuition to a large degree. Learning to use it in your life will give you great results and will allow you to develop your personality to higher levels.

What is Intuition?

Intuition is very hard to define, because it cannot be seen, it is felt. It is about listening to your instincts, listening to your gut feeling. Intuition doesn't rely upon logical thought, it is about tuning into your own thoughts and feelings on something and allowing that to guide you.

You've no doubt heard of Mother's Intuition. This is when a mother knows there is something wrong with her child, without really having any solid evidence to suggest it. Most of the time, this intuition is correct, and it has been used to protect for centuries. We can't study it because we can't measure it, but that doesn't make it any less real.

Think about a situation you have encountered in your life when you simply had a strong feeling about it. Perhaps you were moving house, and you walked into one house ad it just didn't feel right. You walked into another, and it felt right. Did you choose the latter one? Hopefully you did, because this would be your intuition guiding your decision. There is no real scientific or logical evidence to suggest why that happened, but your instincts were telling you that the second house was the best one for you.

Perhaps you have been in a relationship at some point in your life which now no longer exists? And if you're honest with yourself, at times during the relationship you may have experienced doubts about the person or the relationship in some way. At the time you may have justified it with some reasoning in your head or chose to ignore it in some way. Then a few years pass you by and the relationship suddenly ends. You start to remember those 'feelings' of doubt that you once had and the dots start to connect. It's often a clear sign that we didn't listen to our gut in those moments. And more often than not, our gut tends to prove that it is right at some point later down the line.

Intuition can also be as a result of evidence which has occurred in the past, memories of behaviors, and then simply understanding a situation instinctively from that. For instance, hopefully this has never happened to you, but let's give the example. If a partner has cheated on you in the past, you will recognize the signs if it was to happen again. You would see the way they were acting back then, and if it repeated itself, you would become suspicious. You would examine it and try and talk yourself out of it, but the feeling may not go away. Yes, this could be you being paranoid out of fear, but a lot of the time, this simply isn't the case. It could very well be that you found out a little later that your partner was indeed doing the dirty once more. This was your intuition telling you what was likely to be happening.

Intuition can be used in so many different situations, but it can also be harnessed as a guide and decision-making tool too.

What Does Intuition Feel Like?

You usually feel intuition in your gut, in your stomach. This will be a butterfly feeling, a sense of doom, a sense of joy, a sense of 'yes' or 'no'. It's very hard to give an actual description, because it totally depends on the situation and the person. It will simply be the way a situation or place makes you feel.

Try this…

Close your eyes for a second and just try to visualize your intuition. Where is it located? Does it have a color? A shape? What texture is it? Is there a feeling?

If a thought simply won't go away, if it is nagging at you, and you feel a bit sick or giddy whenever you think about it, this is your intuition may be trying to guide you.

If you've not naturally used your intuition much in the past, when you first start to try and tap into it, you might question everything; you might even think that you're overthinking things, or that you're allowing paranoia to sweep in. That could be right, because distinguishing between paranoia, fear, and intuition at first can be very difficult. This is something which will come with practice. The more you use your intuition, the stronger it will be. It's a little like your arm muscles. If you don't go to the gym, you're not going to be able to carry much weight. If you go to the gym, work those muscles out, they will become stronger, and you'll be able to carry more in the future.

Intuition is the same – it needs flexing on occasion.

How Can You Learn to Listen to Your Intuition?

Practice, practice, practice!

If you haven't used your intuition before, or if you've felt it but not acted upon it, it's going to take practice in order to not only use, it but to trust it too. We know that in any friendship or relationship, trust needs to be built up, and the same goes for your budding relationship with your intuition too. It takes time, but once you get there, you'll be able to use your intuition as a guide for big decisions, or simply to know which way is best for you.

Meditation is a great way to learn how to tap into this sixth sense of yours. Meditation is often something people roll their eyes at, but that is because they don't understand it. Meditation doesn't have to be about chanting and going into a trance for hours, it can simply be about quiet contemplation. This is a personal deal, it is whatever works for you.

Try this simple exercise.

Sit down somewhere quiet, when you're not going to be disturbed. Turn off your phone and lock the door. Make sure you're super-comfortable in the clothes you're wearing and the place you're sitting or lying down. It's whatever works for you in this case.

Now, close your eyes and think about your breath. Breathe in slowly through your nose, for a count of five, hold it for two seconds, and then breath out through your mouth, in a controlled and slow manner, for five seconds. Continue this until you feel calm and settled.

If any thought comes into your mind at this point, acknowledge it, and let it drift away, don't pay anything any attention. And don't judge or beat yourself up for the thoughts. They are completely normal.

After a while you will notice that your mind begins to slow down and clear. This will take practice, and the first time you do it you'll probably have a million thoughts trying to get your attention. Don't let that put you off, it's going to take a few tries to get there.

Once you find yourself at that quiet moment, think about the area you want to tap into your intuition on. For example, if you want to move house, picture the house you're thinking of buying or renting, and see how it makes you feel in that moment.

Do you feel good about it? Do you feel unsure still? Is there something which just doesn't feel right, or feels 'off'? This feeling is your intuition.

You can take it a step further by then picturing a specific detail of the house, trying to narrow it down to what exactly feels wrong about it.

By the end of the session, you should have a clearer idea on how you really feel about it, away from the chatter and 'what ifs' that might be clouding up your mind in the normal run of the day.

Again, remember that practice makes perfect here, and that it's not all suddenly going to click into place overnight! Well that's not entirely true actually… Let me rephrase. PERFECT practice makes perfect.

Another way to learn to trust your inner voice is to listen to it and act on it. You'll see that after the first few times of it going well, you'll being to listen to it more and more, rely upon it more and more too. It's the same with anything in life, you only really get a true reflection on whether it works for you, by actually doing it and seeing how it turns out.

5
Develop Your Leadership Skills

As an ENFJ, you are a natural born leader. You are someone that everyone wants on their team, because you have the guts to make things happen!

If you're reading that and thinking 'I'm really not a leader', then this is a chapter you need to pay serious attention to! That leader is in there somewhere, he or she just needs to be let out and run riot for a short while, before you come to realize that yes! You are a leader!

Great leaders don't have to be loud. They don't have to be overpowering. They don't have to lead on major projects and big world-changing events. You're not aiming to become the President. If you are, good luck with it!

No, being a leader is about inspiring others, guiding others, and being a great example. You are all of those things naturally.

Developing your leadership skills is something which will stand you in great stead for the future, especially if you are thinking of making a career move. Even if you're not, being a leader is a positive thing even in everyday life – people will feel they can come to you with their problems, you will be more able to go out and making things happen, your confidence will be greater, and you will create opportunities, which could lead to great places.

What is a Leader?

A true leader is not a dictator, it is not someone who tells people what to do. A true leader doesn't have to be feared, but they do need to be respected. You earn that respect by leading by example and showing the necessary guidance to others.

We mentioned it briefly earlier, but a good leader inspires those who they are leading, they inspire outside of the team they are leading, and they are a point of contact for issues. Leaders are people who others go to for advice and guidance, they are idea generators, they advocate change, and they are a role model-esque person for others to look up and say 'hey, I want to be like that'.

None of this takes great skill for an ESFJ, you simply need to be yourself and allow your leadership qualities to come to the fore. If you're not sure what this entails, you simply follow your intuition (see our last chapter for more on that), and you need to be that example. An example is just by doing the right thing, being a good person – you're already all of those things, so you've got it inside you somewhere! It's about not being afraid to speak up too, and again, you know all about that.

We mentioned that a leader doesn't have to make sweeping changes and rule the world, a leader doesn't have to rule anything, a leader is just someone who offers guidance and an example to other people. Of course, if you want to rule over something, go for it, but if you don't, that's cool too!

The Art of Team Work

Working as a team has so many advantages, and very few disadvantages. This is why most workplaces prefer team working over individual working patterns. You love to talk to others, you're a very sociable person, you're outgoing, and you're always coming up with ideas and routes towards success. This makes you a great team player, and in fact, that is one of the key qualities of an ENFJ personality type.

Being a good team player isn't about taking over, it isn't about being the one in charge, it's about contributing to the overall aim of the team, it's about helping others who might be struggling, it's about offering guidance and inspiration. Again, that's all inside you.

Key Leadership Skills

Now we know what a leader is and what a leader does, we need to identify the key skills and traits of an effective leader. The idea is that by reading this list, you can identify the ones you have already, and also pick out the ones that you need to work on a little. If you can do this, you'll soon find that your leadership skills are enhanced quite quickly.

A good leader:

- Has a quiet confidence, and isn't arrogant or flashy

- Is an inspiration to other people, by being a good role model
- Knows the difference between right and wrong
- Offers a place to go for advice and guidance, completely confidentially
- Is kind and approachable
- Is authentic and doesn't pretend to be something they're not
- Can read people quite well and knows how to adapt their approach to certain personality types, e.g. an introverted person may require a different approach to an extroverted person
- Has passion for the team's overall aim/or for whatever they are leading
- Always comes up with new ideas and approaches
- Seeks out new opportunities
- Is a good listener
- Gives good advice
- Understands that they don't know it all, and is always willing to continue learning and developing
- Is never afraid to ask for advice if they're not sure of something
- Will always stand up for what is right
- Never afraid to speak out in the right circumstances
- Provides a compassionate ear for those who are struggling
- Gently pushes those around them to achieve
- Never lets their feet leave the ground

If you can tick off every item on that list, you're a great leader already. It's likely that there are one or two on there that you need to work on at this point, and that's fine. That's the whole point of this book – to identify areas that you need to work on, to push forward your strengths to a higher level. If you can do that, your leadership skills will be the stuff of legend, will serve you well throughout your life, and allow you to help countless others along the way.

6
Use Your Charisma And Outgoing Nature to Socialize and Network

Our final practical chapter is all about using that charisma and charm to socialize and network, both for business reasons, and personal ones.

We all need to meet people in our lives, for various different reasons. In most cases, it's about making friends and forging relationships, and in other situations it's about meeting people who you can connect with on a business level, in a mutually beneficial arrangement.

You have the skills within you to be able to network very efficiently. You are a sound public speaker, and you possess the subtle knowledge of when to change your tone or language to suit a particular situation, or person. As an ENFJ, we know that you are likely to be always trying to help out some cause or another, and a key way you can achieve the help you need for that endeavor is by networking.

We can't save everyone on our own, sometimes we need a little help!

You are a very warm, authentic, caring, and chatty person, but you're not someone who is likely to be 'in your face'. You have an unarming charm that allows you to gain the trust of most of the people you're speaking to quite quickly. Now, if you can use that to create strong bonds for future business or cause-related issues, surely that's got to be a plus point, right?

Of course!

The Art of Networking

Networking is when a group of like-minded individuals come together at an event and build connections and relationships. It's a great opportunity for people to share business contact details and to build up a list of connections in a range of different professions. For instance, if you were looking to set up a fundraising event for animals in need, you could look back on any people you met in the past who had a link to animal welfare or cruelty. You could also think if there were any contacts related to raising awareness for various causes or any PR people.

This is not about meeting people for a particular aim in the future, but about building up a catalogue of people who you can, of course, socialize with if you want to, but also call upon in the future for a mutual favor. They can then call you if they need something which you specialize in.

This is the art of networking, and it is something which has been done for decades.

In order to network, you need to go to events and speak. Of course, you can also network when you're in the local supermarket, it depends who you bump into! Have your contact details handy at all times, so it might be worth having a printed business card in your bag, which you can give out if you meet someone who has connections to a particular cause or issue that you feel you could help with, or who could help you. Your business card doesn't need to be fancy, it just needs to have your name, telephone number, email address on. That's it. Yu can easily make these for free with downloadable apps these days! There is no need for expensive print services anymore.

Of course, the more you get out and about, the more networking you can do. This means going to any events that are relevant, any charity fairs, local fairs, that kind of thing. The more you get out and give your contact details, the more you will receive back. This could all turn out to be very beneficial to you in the future, when you're trying to bring awareness to a cause, or arrange an event of your own.

You could also have an online presence on relevant forums online too. Networking doesn't have to be done in person, it can be done virtually, just as successfully. So, look at reputable forums which deal with the types of situations or causes you're involved in, and participate in conversations or debates. You never know what kind of help or advice you might find, and your outgoing nature should make this quite easy for you too.

The Importance of Socializing – We All Need a Circle

Before we finish up our practical chapters, remember this one piece of advice – you are not an island!

You are such a warm, caring, friendly, and genuine person on the inside that you should have a whole circle of friends upon whom you can rely and call for random days or nights out. Perhaps you do, and in that case, well done, that's great! If you don't, this isn't likely to be anything reflecting badly on you at all, it's probably that you just don't have the time to socialize!

Make the time. It's that simple. We all need a circle, and we all need time to relax. By doing this, you will actually enrich the lives of others, with your warm and friendly nature, and you'll get a support system out of it too.

Conclusion

And there we have it, we've come to the end of our fascinating journey into the key workings of an ENFJ personality type.

We've learnt all about the fantastic strengths you possess, and we've talked about how to maximize their effects too. By this point, you should be feeling uplifted, and ready to start your own personal development journey. This will be one of the greatest, if not the greatest, journeys you will ever take.

Remember, if you're not sure if one particular point is relevant to you, make sure you study on that point more than the others. This is probably a trait which you have inside you and needs to be encourage to come out! Some you might not need to work on quite so much, because they're already there. It's about identifying how much work you need to do as an individual, because we're all so different.

We're sure you'll agree that learning about personality types is a really interesting and fascinating subject. You could try and encourage your friends and family to take the Myers-Briggs test too, to find out what their core type is. From there, you can learn more about how they tick on the inside, and that could help you to understand them much more. This may then help you to tailor your responses and approach to them in the future.

Remember to check out the other personality types which you believe you resonate with closely too. We're rarely 100% in one camp, so it's a good idea to check out the surrounding types too, to give you a more complete overview, and a more rewarding journey to completeness!

All that is left is for us to wish you luck in your ENFJ self-development journey. Read through each section as many times as you need, and if you're still not sure, read over it again! Try out the exercises we've talked about and focus your time on the sections that you feel you need to concentrate on more. This is not a race, but a journey that will take as long as it needs to take. We are never too old or too experienced to learn something new, and by remembering that fact, you really do hold the key to greater experiences and opportunities in the future.

If you'd like to learn more about developing your weaknesses, you can get my other book - ENFJ: Understand And Break Free From Your Own Limitations. But for now, let's get back to business and focus on your powers.

Note from the author

Thank you for purchasing and reading this book. If you enjoyed it or found it useful then I'd really appreciate it if you would post a short review on Amazon. I do read all the reviews personally so that I can continually write what people are wanting.

If you'd like to leave a review then please visit the link below:

https://www.amazon.com/dp/B07CZPRXNP

Thanks for your support and good luck!

Check Out My Other Books

Below you'll find some of my other books that are popular on Amazon and Kindle as well. Simply search the titles listed below on Amazon. Alternatively, you can visit my author page on Amazon to see other work done by me.

ENFP: Understand and Break Free From Your Own Limitations

INFP: Understand and Break Free From Your Own Limitations

ENFJ: Understand and Break Free From Your Own Limitations

INFJ: Understand and Break Free From Your Own Limitations

ENFP: INFP: ENFJ: INFJ: Understand and Break Free From Your Own Limitations – The Diplomat Bundle Series

INTP: Understand and Break Free From Your Own Limitations

INTJ: Understand and Break Free From Your Own Limitations

ENTP: Understand and Break Free From Your Own Limitations

ENTJ: Understand and Break Free From Your Own Limitations

ESTJ: Understand and Break Free From Your Own Limitations

ISTJ: Understand and Break Free From Your Own Limitations

ISFJ: Understand and Break Free From Your Own Limitations

ESFJ: Understand and Break Free From Your Own Limitations

ISFP: Understand and Break Free From Your Own Limitations

ESTP: Understand and Break Free From Your Own Limitations

ISTP: Understand and Break Free From Your Own Limitations

OPTION B: F**K IT - How to Finally Take Control Of Your Life And Break Free From All Expectations. Live A Limitless, Fearless, Purpose Driven Life With Ultimate Freedom

Printed in Great Britain
by Amazon